*F*ANTASY, ADULTERY AND A YEAR of sheer emotional turmoil occurred in the life of an ordinary woman who made some extra ordinary life choices. Certainly there was rapturous pleasure, yet as the tale unfolded, the outcome was one which no one could have possibly foreseen.

This unlikely and difficult pathway would lead to the creation of a new woman. Not a new female species with super powers, but a very human woman who could finally love and accept herself. A woman who could celebrate her successes, learn from her mistakes and who could triumphantly confess that her heart was now whole.

Confessions of an Unfaithful Heart

by

ALISON L. TINSLEY

authorHOUSE®

AuthorHouse™ UK Ltd.
500 Avebury Boulevard
Central Milton Keynes, MK9 2BE
www.authorhouse.co.uk
Phone: 08001974150

©2008 Alison L. Tinsley. All rights reserved.

No part of this book may be reproduced, stored in a retrieval system, or transmitted by any means without the written permission of the author.

First published by AuthorHouse 9/2/2008

ISBN: 978-1-4343-9491-0 (sc)

Printed in the United States of America
Bloomington, Indiana

This book is printed on acid-free paper.

To my family, friends and associates who have believed in me, inspired me and encouraged me to exceed my expectations. Thank you with all my heart.

Alison x

Contents

Chapter One	1
Yesterday	
Chapter Two	13
Someday My Prince Will Come	
Chapter Three	23
One Night in Heaven	
Chapter Four	35
When Will I See You Again?	
Chapter Five	43
There's No Place like Home	
Chapter Six	53
I Want to Break Free	
Chapter Seven	71
Starting Over	
Chapter Eight	79
Single	

Introduction

I HAVE A CONFESSION TO MAKE. Let me explain. My story begins over twelve years ago, I was a different woman then. Like so many people, I was unaware that much of my life revolved around searching for love and approval. And yet you could say I had it all, a husband, two great kids, a strong faith, a fulfilling career and a lovely home. So why did I feel so empty, so lonely and so desperate to be loved?

Why indeed? At the time I didn't have any answers, only an incredibly strong, subconscious need, to be valued and appreciated for who I was. My marriage of eleven years had been a happy one, but it had arrived at a place where many marriages visit, a place called 'familiarity'. Movies like 'Pretty Woman' simply fuelled my fantasies. I wanted my own Richard Gere to pull up outside my house, in his white limousine, to rescue me from the curse of monotony. Little did I understand the power of my day dreams. I was soon to discover the difference between Hollywood and real life.

Herein lies my story, a journey through fantasy, adultery and ultimately, self–discovery. Subsequent events would change my life, forever. My actions prompted a year of sheer emotional turmoil. Certainly there was rapturous pleasure; forbidden fruit does something quite tantalizing to the taste buds. And yet as my tale unfolded, the outcome was one which I could not possibly have foreseen. Once my foot had taken its first step across the line of temptation, there would be no going back, no return to normality and life would never be the same again.

So why would I want to share such a story? Well, my hope is that it will help and inspire others. So many struggle with the same issues as I did, low self esteem, lack of confidence and an inability to accept oneself. As you read my story, I trust you will open your mind. Try to understand and, more importantly, apply the lessons learnt from my mistakes. If you can do this, then your life can take on new and exciting possibilities, no longer confined by the constraints of your past or your mind.

We are all under such pressure from the media, peers, and society. It's a subtle but relentless pressure to feel inadequate unless we have it all. Many hair and beauty manufacturers would have us believe we deserve to have their products. The irony is that we are indeed worth far more than we realise, but having more things and looking young forever will not satisfy that inner craving for happiness and peace. I was just one victim who was sucked into this lie, an ordinary woman who apparently had it all, yet one who made some extraordinary life choices. This unlikely and difficult pathway would lead to the creation of a new woman. Not a new female species with super powers, but a very human woman who could finally love and accept herself. A woman who could celebrate her successes, learn from her mistakes and who could triumphantly confess that her heart was now whole.

I trust you enjoy the story and learn as much about living life to the full as I have.

Lavishly yours,

Alison x

Chapter One

Yesterday

My eyes opened slowly, gradually becoming aware of the morning sun peeping through the faded curtains. In the sunshine, even the glistening dust seemed to enjoy being carried merrily along. The sound of distant church bells, chiming softly, heralded the start of a new day. I began to wonder what sort of day it would be, the warmth of the sun already giving me cause to believe it would be a good one. But before I was able to indulge my thoughts further, a sudden chill crept along my spine and my heart began to race. Only a few minutes passed, though it felt more like a lifetime. The recent and painful turbulent events came flooding back into my mind. How could something so invigorating, so passionate and all encompassing, have turned into this confusing disarray, leaving behind a trail of heartbreak, desolation, and pain?

Just months previously, my life seemed, to the outside world at least, quite idyllic. I loved my work in the nursing profession, which I found intensely rewarding. A meaningful church life added a spiritual dimension to my day-to-day living. My marriage of eleven years was to a man with a stable career, who loved me the best way he knew how. I had married at the tender age of twenty. Like so many young women of this age, I believed I held all knowledge, all wisdom, and that the whole world was my oyster. My parents had held reservations about my marrying so young, but why did they think they had the monopoly on what was best for me? After all, when I met my husband-to-be, he was the image of the delectable Les Mckeown. (For those of you too young to remember, Les was the lead singer of the immensely talented Bay City Rollers.

They were the tartan-clad band singing "bye bye baby, baby, bye bye"). Anyway, I thought he was amazingly sexy, and I was only fifteen. Of course my parents disapproved, but what did they know about pop? They thought modern music was still being sung by Gene Pitney (sorry, Gene).

I recall the first heart-stopping moments after my eyes fell upon the dreamy figure of the Les Mckeown double. His charm was irresistible as he stood in work-worn overalls, the toils of the day very apparent. It didn't matter that he was obviously ready for a hot bath and that his thick, dark locks needed a shampoo. Neither did the rather unglamorous surroundings of the southern bus station detract from my amorous Les gazing. All I could see was a dark, handsome guy who seemed to tick all my boxes in the quest for love. Of course, I didn't know anything about him, but at fifteen who cares? As teenagers, many of us are a little superficial and concerned more with a boyfriend's outer appearance than his character.

Having set my stall out to catch this Bay City Roller, I had to work out a plan to meet him. By chance, I saw him speaking with someone who regularly caught my own bus. What luck. I decided to ask this friend to introduce us. It sounds awfully pushy now, but at the time I just wanted my man. And so it was that the unsuspecting 'Les' and I were introduced by our mutual friend a few days later. It turned out his name wasn't 'Les,' but Gary, and he was an electrician at the railway works, hence the somewhat dishevelled appearance after work. We chatted for a short while and Gary seemed to like me. I knew

I liked him already. Eventually we arranged to go on a date together. How exciting!

Our first get-together went well, and one date led to another and another and another. I had become quite besotted with Gary. Indeed he was very attractive and my friends were a little jealous, although they wouldn't admit it. Our courtship lasted five years and had its fair share of romance and fun, as well as the routine that longer lasting relationships bring. By and large we were very well suited and genuinely cared for each other. Both ambitious and career minded, with a shared love of sport and cars, we had a great deal going for us.

Gary could be quite romantic at times. I remember on one of our first Christmases together, he bought a gigantic cuddly St Bernard toy dog for me. He was uncharacteristically animated as he gave me his gift. Even his mother thought it a lovely gesture. We used little imagination in naming him Bernie, but he was a constant source of affection for many years.

And so it was that, despite a warning about being too young, too head strong, and too stupid to listen, I married anyway. As it happened, I was very much in love with my lead singer look-alike, and I believe he was in love with me. What girl wouldn't want to marry a tall (well, 5 feet 10 inches), dark, handsome man with great career prospects and fabulous hair? (Why is it that so many blokes have such a thick crop and we girls often have so little?) It wasn't just his hair that appealed to me; his personal qualities weren't bad either—reliable, ambitious, hard working, at times comical, and his attention to detail second to none. At times he bore the hallmarks of a perfectionist, but since I wasn't that far behind in this respect, I chose not to let this bother me.

Perhaps the only down side of his personality, as I saw it, was his temper. Especially if anything happened to his precious first car (an old Toyota Corolla, which he had lovingly restored and held in great admiration). Once his wrath was aroused, I thought he gave *the* most lifelike impression of the Incredible Hulk I have ever seen. I remember once, when I was learning to drive at age seventeen, I stalled *his* car three times. He had been so patient up to that point but, on the third engine stop at a junction, before even he knew it, the big green giant was aroused for a virtuoso performance! I was so upset, I abandoned the car and ran off down the central reservation of the carriageway. It must have seemed most bizarre for the onlooker, not to mention rather dangerous. The verdant creature having retreated, my husband chased after me, proclaiming his apology with as much fervour as the anger that had caused the original offence.

Overall, he was a lovely man, with a kind heart and gentle spirit (mostly). He was a man who enjoyed his sport, the quiet life, and the occasional pint. Even in the eighties, when we married, it was quite uncommon to have had only one sexual partner. Quite sweet really, and so was our marriage. Even before our wedding, my husband had performed acts of courage and loving chivalry. I recall how he made an appointment to speak with my father to ask for my hand in marriage. Nothing too unusual in that, you may think. However, if I explain that my parents had taken a dislike to him early in our relationship

(I think they thought he was too old for me) and then refused to let him in the house, it puts the enormity of his request into proportion. He showed great bravery; indeed, it was his honourable behaviour that won my parents over in the end.

This attitude of care and concern carried on into our marriage. Indeed comments were made long after the honeymoon period about how much in love we were, how proud I was of him, and what a handsome couple we were. He excelled in that one area where we girls all want such expertise and supremacy—you've guessed it—D. I. Y! It was pure joy to observe his unending talents with a Bosch drill. I was the envy of other wives, whose husbands hadn't mastered the art of the erection of the kitchen cupboard.

This harmonious union gave me great pleasure and fulfilment, at least in our early years together. I enjoyed making our small but detached house into a home that we were immensely proud of. Like so many other couples, we both worked our little socks off trying to earn enough brass to pay that never-ending round of household bills, bills such as the dastardly mortgage and the extortionate car payment. Holidays were somewhat of a luxury. Even our honeymoon had been in Wales (not that there is anything wrong with Wales, but Paris would have been nice).

This sense of building a life together drew us closer, and we did seem to have a good understanding of one another. Indeed, my husband was incredibly tolerant of my rather unusual pet rabbit, Timothy Donny Delicious Mr Nibble Barlow. (If you're really interested you can e-mail me and I'll explain the name in full!) As pets go, he really was a star. Chosen on my tenth birthday, he appeared unique from the beginning, being able to respond to his name, beg for food, virtually live in the house, and even lick my tears on many an occasion. Often I would set little jumps made from old bricks and my Dads' garden canes, place him in a cat harness, and off we would go, cavorting round the garden like a scene from *Alice in Wonderland*. As the years rolled by, Timbo, as my Dad fondly called him, and I became quite an item. Those who knew of him only by name often mistook him for my boyfriend. I had considered having him at our wedding, with his white fur beautifully groomed and a blue ribbon tied neatly in a bow around his dainty nape. However, there were those who deemed it inappropriate. I still can't see why! So it was that my husband married a woman, not with a bun in the oven but with a bunny as her love. No mean feat for any man, let alone one originating from Barnsley! (For those of you unfamiliar with this mining town in South Yorkshire, some might say it is the very heart of the male macho ego.)

Apart from tolerating my funny little idiosyncrasies, my husband tried hard to keep me happy. Before I bought my first car, I relied on him and public transport to get to and from work. He never seemed to mind, even when the hour was very late or very early. And when it came to buying my first car, he encouraged me to choose well, and I did – an MG Midget with soft top. Exhilarating does not even come close to describing the many adventures I experienced in the five years as its proud owner.

As befits the owner of a red sports car, the years of marital bliss literally sped by. Soon the patter of tiny feet became a familiar sound in our home (no, not the rabbit). We had two fantastic children who meant the world to me. I loved taking care of them. One of my favourite 'Mumsy' roles was helping them with their reading when they were very young. Seeing them develop their reading skills, from imaginative descriptions of wordless stories to often quite hilarious attempts to read 'look', 'where', and 'house', certainly warmed the heart. The rapturous euphoria expressed by a child on the completion of a book is quite contagious, isn't it?

When it came to learning to spell, they gave just as much pleasure with their wonderfully courageous attempts. I remember my daughter, at about four years of age, asking how to spell a certain word whilst we were all on a long car journey. At first I didn't understand what she meant by the question,

'Mummy, how do you spell "ponna"?'

'What do you mean, sweetheart?' I replied. 'I don't think there is such a word.'

'But there is, Mummy, I've heard it lots of times,' she said as indignantly as it is possible to sound at such an early age. Her next sentence would reveal the mystery word and its uncertain origin.

'When you read me a story Mummy, you nearly always start with "Once u ponna time...."'

And there it was, the simple logic of a childlike mind. Such a shame we seem to lose it as the years go by.

As they grew older, the innocence of their tiny minds developed into something far more alarming. Utter bedlam often ensued when trying to get two children to rouse from a slumber so deep, they might as well have been on planet Vulcan. It was most disconcerting to find that even when their eyes finally opened and their bodies were in the upright position, an alien-sounding, monosyllabic grunt emitted from their mouths. Their body movements added further credence to a terrifying suspicion; had my beloved offspring indeed been abducted by aliens and replaced with imbecilic replicas? Fortunately, by lunchtime, the extra-terrestrial thieves had usually returned their captives, although on one or two occasions they seemed to have held them for a whole weekend!

With the arrival of our children, previously peaceful teatimes presented us with a conflict – healthy eating versus convenience. I would love to say that the freshly prepared, wholesome variety of meals won the day. More often than not, however, it was whatever I could lay my hands on in the freezer. Usually it was cardboard-tasting pizza with hard black bullets (allegedly olives), soggy oven chips, and that age old favourite, the baked bean, with its ever enduring and lingering after-effects.

By this time, I had moved from hospital nursing into a role as practice nurse. It had been a personal dream to achieve this position and gave me great pleasure and satisfaction. In fact, it had taken seven years of being turned down at interviews (because I didn't have the relevant experience) before I was finally offered this idyllic post. It's a good job I didn't give in at the first hurdle. Little did I know that learning to persevere was a quality that would help see me through the difficult times that lay ahead.

Working in a Yorkshire Dales practice, the conversation would often revolve around the reproductive capabilities of sheep, Mrs Jones's infected toenail (again), and poor Sister White's husband's broken leg. Oh, and let's not forget the obligatory chunterings about the renowned doctor's receptionist. (In reality, where would we be without them? Up the creek without a paddle – or even a boat – I'm sure.)

I could recall many a humorous story. I will recount just one, which still amuses me to this day. One of my roles was to give healthy eating advice and provide a 'weigh in' clinic. Many patients attended, some lost all the weight they needed to, many didn't. Some, I am sorry to say, even gained a few pounds. One particular lady sticks in my mind, because she took to heart every piece of advice I gave her. One of the tips I used for cutting down on the amount of food eaten at mealtimes was to use a smaller plate. So instead of a dinner plate, I suggested she use a dessert plate. At her next appointment two weeks later, she entered the treatment room with an old holdall. I thought nothing of it at the time, as elderly ladies often brought large shopping bags with them. Perhaps it was an old Yorkshire custom to visit the doctor's with the kitchen sink in their bags? I'm still not quite sure to this day. Anyway, whatever the tradition, I proceeded with the consultation. She was delighted when, upon stepping off the scales, I informed her that she had lost three pounds. Her face lit up and then she walked over to the holdall and proceeded to unzip it.

"You mentioned last time about the size of my plate," she eagerly informed me.

"I wanted to show you the size, just to be sure," she explained, as she carefully presented me with a fine china dessert plate. Seeing the size of the bag, I began to wonder what else 'she had brought to show me just to be sure'. Had she brought the food that sat on this daintily proportioned plate as well? Fortunately not, and the bag's other contents weren't for my eyes, so I reassured her that the size was just right and she was doing a splendid job in her fight to lose weight. In fact, she went on to reach her target weight. Well done, Plate Lady!

And so my life chugged merrily along on this road we all call 'marital bliss'. To the passer-by at least, my life could be compared to a BMW 3 series – with leather upholstery, remote controlled sunroof, CD player, and satellite navigation system. Let's face it, I had a faithful husband, two fabulous children, a lovely home, and a great job. So why did I feel so unloved and so unhappy?

Chapter Two

Someday My Prince Will Come

I suppose, at some time or another, most married people have felt the way I did. After many years of marriage, the familiar can become rather boring, and the endless routine becomes a little mundane. I'm sure you know what I am talking about. The alarm clock rings in its usual, irritating way, followed by several attempts to switch it off with an arm that doesn't seem to belong to you. Rummaging can be heard at the other side of the bed.

'Where did you put my undies, love?' grunts the sleepy creature you vaguely recall being sexually intimate with the night before. He wasn't worried where his undies were then. In fact, he couldn't wait to get them off!

By the time your face has been washed, the day does seem a little more welcoming, your partner a little more human. After making sure the children and hubby have eaten breakfast and put their clothes on in the right order and the right way around (yes, I still include hubby at this point), it's time to leave for work. But before you leave, there's the washing machine to load and the dishes to wash. There's just enough time to nip to the loo, and then disaster strikes – your ring catches your tights and causes an enormous ladder. Typically it's in a place the whole world can see, between your knee and ankle. By now your stress levels are rising; you're feeling anxious and wondering how you are going to make it to work on time. But like the wonder woman you are, you somehow manage it. By the time you get into the car after dropping the children off at school or the childminder, a huge sigh of relief slips unconsciously through your lips. At last, peace and quiet.

Some time to think before taking on another load of demands at your place of work or the endless chores in your unpaid role as wife and mother.

That car journey can be quite a haven. Your choice of music playing at the volume you like. Driving at the speed you want without an anxious husband or twittering children telling you, '*Please* slow down, love!' or 'Mum, can't you go any faster?' (I actually enjoy driving rather fast.) These car journeys allowed my imagination to run riot, and I would dream of endless exciting possibilities to brighten up my mundane life. I had no idea some of my thoughts would become reality. At this stage, I did not understand the power of the unconscious mind. Nor did I realize that we are pulled towards, and become like, what we focus on most. What a pity I had no inkling of how my mind worked; it would have saved an awful lot of pain and upheaval. And so, upon arrival at work, my wandering thoughts were brought into dock until they could be re-floated later.

As with most careers, there are good days and, well, days that aren't. I am pleased to report that most of mine were the former. In fact, I loved my job. As I have already said, I had wanted to be a practice nurse for many years. It had taken a great amount of patience and perseverance to land this post. It had taken me around seven years, four interviews, and much new experience gained before I managed to secure the position I had dreamed of. I was, if nothing else, persistent!

Being a practice nurse gave me great satisfaction. As soon as I put my uniform on, I felt worthy of respect and had a part to play in society. It wasn't until years later that I realised my uniform had become an actor's costume. I could hide behind it and play the sort of role I really wanted. My personality was the same – a bubbly blonde who smiled a great deal – but my self esteem rose to unprecedented heights as I acted out my part with earnest.

Sometimes patients would misinterpret my enthusiasm, and many an elderly gentleman took a shine to me. On one occasion a retired gent, whom I had seen many times and who was always a little too friendly, made a dash for me and kissed me on the lips! It's amazing how quickly a so-called OAP can dart across a room at the prospect of kissing a blonde. After that, I made sure his appointments were with a different nurse.

At other times my patients were the most kind and generous people imaginable. One lady would bring chocolates at every visit, while another gave all the nurses a gift voucher one Christmas. I bought a china teapot with a chintz pattern and still treasure it to this day.

And so it was that my life jollied along. Marriage, kids, work, and the annual holiday. My husband said he loved me, but if evidence was needed to prove it in court, I am not sure he would have had a case. I had become increasingly aware of a deep need to be loved and valued, a need that my husband was not fulfilling. Over the previous few years, it seemed to me I wasn't worth the effort anymore.

I remember on my thirtieth birthday sensing that something wasn't quite right. All day, I was thinking that he had arranged something special – he seemed so withdrawn I was positive he was keeping a secret. A surprise party perhaps? I waited in anticipation for him to ask me to get ready, to put on something sparkly, and then whisk me away. I had a bath and did my hair just in case. It wasn't until my friend rang in the evening to wish me happy birthday and ask if I was doing anything that I realised I wasn't doing anything at all.

The birth of my daughter brought more disappointment. I was on one of those ghastly hospital beds. You know the sort – the starched sheets were newly laundered and scratchy and the plastic mattress had me sweating. Gary was having trouble keeping his eyes open. The ward was dimly lit and quiet, as it was the early hours of the morning. There was no one around.

'The pains are worsening,' I groaned to Gary, and he just grunted his acknowledgement. I rang the call buzzer to summon the midwife. No one came. The contractions were becoming stronger.

'Gary,' I cried. Panic and distress overcame any reservation I had left. The time for gentle groaning was long gone. Gary still slumbered on. My anguish intensified. Despite the stickiness, I managed to disengage myself from the mattress. The sheet came with me, dangling between my cheeks, clinging and trailing behind. What a picture! A particularly vicious contraction bent me double. I tried one last time to rouse my husband.

'Gary! I need your help.'

Gary slumbered on. Just when I needed him. I saw this as yet another example of his regard for me, or lack of it. Sticky and in terrible pain, I went in search of help elsewhere.

After the birth of our first child, a son, Gary was to provide the meals during those first shell shocked days at home. Unfortunately his culinary skills did not match those in his D. I. Y repertoire. His toad in the hole would have been put to better use in his tool shed as cement!

I spent my first day home in my nighty because I didn't have a chance to get my clothes on. The whole time revolved around the needs of our new baby. Utterly exhausted due to the feeding, burping, and changing of endless nappies of black runny poo, I repeatedly asked myself, 'What on Earth is going on, and will life ever be normal again?' Perhaps most new mums think the same; otherwise, you'd have to be perfect.

After the first weekend of sleepless nights, sore nipples, and constipation, I just wanted to send the crying creature back to where it had come from! Fortunately my son soon settled down to four hours of sleep at night, and with at least some slumber under my belt, I was able to tackle motherhood without the aid of matchsticks!

I do remember however, that on our return home from hospital with our beautiful newborn daughter, Gary had made a big effort. Gary tried really hard with the cooking, and his attempts to tickle my taste buds were vastly improved. No need for the tool shed this time.

Perhaps I should have focused more on Gary's improved kitchen efforts, as it wasn't long before I began to feel undervalued and unloved. Further episodes, behaviours, and words caused to me to believe my husband did not appreciate me or think I was worth the effort of loving.

The incident that finally brought things to a head was a small thing really. You could say it was the proverbial 'straw' that broke the camel's back. It happened during Christmas of 1994. We didn't have a great deal of surplus money, so Gary and I decided we would spend only £10 on each other. Now, I know what you are going to say: Yes, women are from Venus and men are from Mars, and it was naive of me to think that just because I wasn't going to stick to the agreed spending limit that he wasn't either. In case you haven't worked it out, I spent much more than £10 on my husband, while my husband stuck rigidly to the deal. As a result, my Christmas present of 1994 was a video of Disney's *Snow White and the Seven Dwarves*! Yes, I had said I would like a copy, but I didn't expect it to be my only present. In my mind were images of exotic perfume, pretty jewellery, and perhaps sensual underwear, all beautifully wrapped in delicate tissue and ribbon. What was I thinking of? I asked myself sarcastically. After all, we had been married for eleven years. I hadn't realised that wives were not supposed to expect thoughtful gifts after such a length of time.

This occurrence seems quite trivial now, but combined with all the previous 'offenses' it spoke volumes. It screamed to me, with a resonating boom, *'You are not worth any more than a child's video. You are not worth the love and affection of a husband. This Christmas, after eleven years of marriage, you do not deserve a husband's thoughtful gift'.* I remember being quite stunned and feeling an enormous sense of hurt and rejection. I had worked so hard at making my family's Christmas a joyous occasion. Why could my husband not do the same for me? He used to make much more of an effort, but this year's gift seemed such a cold and heartless gesture. Had our marriage come to this? Disney on ice.

He argued that he hadn't done anything wrong, that he had only done what we had agreed upon. But the film seemed to symbolise the state of our cold marriage. I know some of you might think this is normal behaviour for a husband and I was making a huge fuss about nothing. But at that time, I was a woman who needed to be loved, valued, and appreciated. After many previous instances of feeling rejected, I was at rock bottom again. We each have our different thresholds and I had reached mine.

I wasn't particularly looking for what happened next. Indeed, it was the last thing I expected someone of my background would do. But I was vulnerable. I needed to be loved. I wanted to feel the warmth and tenderness of a man who cherished me. I longed for the passion and excitement of a man whose being was totally consumed with desire for me. I had no idea I was capable of my next move.

Chapter Three

One Night in Heaven

*I*N ONE SENSE, I STEPPED out of character. In another, perhaps this was who I really was. At the time, I had no idea. All I knew was that I had become very attracted to a young man, Steve, who had been interested in me for nearly a year. When I say 'interested', I don't mean that he did or said anything, but when he would look at me, his deep brown eyes would take in every move, every curve of my body. Sometimes, just for a moment, our eyes would meet and I would feel irresistibly drawn into a chiasmic pool of utter excitement. On one occasion, our bare arms accidentally touched, and I felt the warmth of his tender skin against mine. A fleeting thought went hurtling through my mind, and I wondered how the rest of his young, naked body would feel gently brushing up against mine. My cheeks flushed, and as quickly as the thought had appeared, the shame that followed took it away. His cheeky smile, with those full, sensual lips, beckoned a passionate response from mine. His whole body language seemed to whisper that he adored me, he wanted me, and he intended to have me.

Even now, it surprises me that Steve and I met at our local church. Many Christians believe they are impervious to the world's moral pitfalls. They think temptation is beyond them and there is no need to be on guard, that emotions magically become controllable when one decides to follow God. What a pity I was one of those naive believers. If only I had been aware that, despite my spiritual awakening, my humanity was still very much intact. If I had been, perhaps I would not have succumbed to Steve's sexual attraction. His youthful ruggedness and seemingly dangerous lifestyle might not have been quite so appealing. At the very least, if I had known Christians were just as capable of giving in to temptation as anyone else, I might have prepared differently. Who knows what I would have done to guard against what happened next? But because of my ignorance I was unprepared.

After the *Snow White* fiasco just a few weeks previously, my resistance to such charm was at an all time low. I suppose you could say we were flirting with each other. Rational thinking and morality were losing their hold on me. I could feel myself being pulled headlong towards someone who was totally devoted to me and whose thoughts were filled with adoration. There was no comparison with the familiar round of monotonous, unimaginative mattress dancing and the perpetual feeling of being taken for granted. My self-esteem was at an all time low, and my need to be valued, loved, and appreciated at an all time high. Well, what was a girl to do?

If I told you he was only twenty years old and I thought of him as a likable rogue, would that surprise you? What about his career? To date, it, had consisted of various low paying jobs with little or no prospects, but who's interested in what someone *does* when they make you *feel* fabulous? Would you be shocked to learn he had a reputation for being a womaniser? He held captive those who watched him as he moved his lithe and toned body to the rhythmic beat on a dance floor, like a nineties version of John Travolta. Had my dancing been better, I could have been his Stephanie. His youth and fashionable dress sense enticed me into believing I could feel young again. I began to think that the responsibilities and weight that came automatically with marriage, children, and a career would lift in his presence.

And so, despite his dubious reputation, I realised that I was being totally drawn in by his compelling infatuation for me. It had been so long since anyone had seen me as a desirable and attractive woman that I could not control my emotions any longer. I realised I was falling in love with this youth's passion for me. I longed to be held by a man whose whole being yearned for mine. The strength of my feelings was overwhelming. I found it was now impossible to resist any longer.

Steve appeared to have had no idea how I felt or how delicate my marriage was. And since his own plans were not working out as he had hoped, Steve made an earth shattering announcement. He had decided to move away to France to live and work with his brother, who had gone out there some years ago and now had a French wife and a family. I must admit, it sounded idyllic. From Steve's perspective, a life in the French countryside would mean good wine, good food, and great French lovers!

At first I was devastated by his revelation. My fanciful thoughts and where they had taken me had come to a sudden stop. My dreams were not going to come true after all, and I wasn't going to embark on an exquisitely pleasurable all-round excursion. (I use the term 'all-round excursion' because I intended to return, despite where the journey might have taken me.)

Then, a delectable, yet daring, thought came into my mind. Steve was leaving the country anyway, so what if I confided in him and revealed my true feelings? It would be our secret, a lovers' secret. What harm could it do? He was moving away, a long way away. So what damage would be caused by one night of indulgence? One night of insatiable delight and rapture? After all, I would never see him again. Well, probably not.

I became giddy at the prospect of what had now become my decided course of action. My heart beat with renewed excitement as I picked up the phone and made the call. I asked Steve if I could take him to a nightclub as my good-bye gift. His reply sounded a little surprised, but he seemed as eager as I was to spend an evening together. The time and venue were agreed upon. It was done. It was actually going to happen. We were going out together, alone.

I somehow persuaded my unsuspecting husband that I was taking Steve out as a farewell gesture before his departure for France. He seemed a little surprised but reluctantly agreed to let me go. Since he believed Steve would be permanently out of the picture perhaps he felt no harm could be done. Whatever my husband's thoughts were, I was thrilled at the prospect of my 'date' with Steve, though a little uncomfortable with the guilt I was also experiencing. However, I rationalized that if my husband really loved me, I wouldn't have been in this position anyway.

After Steve and I arranged the date, I felt ecstatic. My emotions had been reawakened. A breathless exuberance now consumed my thoughts and desires. I don't know how I survived that monumentally long week, but survive I did. The eagerly anticipated evening finally arrived. So many pleasurable thoughts had passed through my mind, more to do with emotional fulfilment than full blown sex. For me, sex without love was empty and meaningless. But I hoped the night would live up to all my expectations. I made every effort to look as attractive as I could. I spent an absolute age on my hair, nails, and makeup until they were perfect – well as perfect as I could make them. Eye shadow never was my strong point. Neither was giving my hair that elusive 'lift' that professionals managed so effortlessly. But as I checked the final look in the mirror, I must admit, I was delighted with the woman who smiled seductively back at me. She appeared quite youthful, sexy even, with an air of elegance. What a pity her own husband didn't seem to see her in this light. However, this was not the night to dwell on *that* fact. This was the night where dreams became reality and one heart would be captured by another.

Driving to the nightclub was a mixture of intense delight and strange unease. Having been with one man for over eleven years, I hadn't realised that I would feel a little uncomfortable with someone else. However, once we arrived at the Blue Moon club and entered together, I slowly began to feel more relaxed. As Steve approached the bar for our drinks, my doting eyes rested on his deliciously buttock hugging jeans, and I knew then that I had been bewitched. He bought me a martini and we sat and chatted about, well, all sorts really. The weather, fashion, cars, sport, and anything else that took our minds off the undeniable feelings we held for each other. There was an enthralling fascination between us and a magnetic force that drew us closer and closer. Each time our eyes met, I felt unable to resist what felt like a promiscuous pool of melting milk chocolate, probably Thorntons Continentals!

After a while, he stood, then took my hand and asked me to dance. My quivering legs almost didn't make it, but as elegantly as I could, I rose to my feet and hand in hand we slowly walked over to the dance floor. Just the touch of his gentle, soft palm on mine was enough to make my heart race once again. The pulsating beat of the music seemed to reflect my own heart's throbbing desire. Steve's body moved and writhed licentiously and effortlessly with the rhythm of the night. Such a shame that my own dancing was more like that of a stiff and starchy accountant with a brush handle up her back! I'm relieved to say that Steve didn't seem to mind.

Steve was such a gentleman. He allowed me to dictate the pace of the evening. I didn't feel rushed or pressured to be someone I wasn't. As we danced, he gently eased his arms around my waist and drew me closer to him. For the first time I could feel his sensual body pressing against mine. In time with the music, he slowly ran his fingers up and down my back, occasionally brushing them through my hair. My head found itself resting on his youthful shoulder, and we moved and swayed together as two people in complete oneness with each other. To the observer, there must have been something quite sweet and innocent about the image before their eyes. It felt that way, too. I was pleasantly surprised at how right it felt at the same time that it felt so wrong.

The evening seemed to transcend time, as if we were in another world. I was determined to squeeze every drop of enjoyment from my night with Steve. As we sat together enjoying another beer and cocktail, I found myself revealing my innermost thoughts about him. How I had become increasingly aware of his feelings for me, that I was so lonely, craved affection and love, and that I could no longer resist his warmth and adoration. Once I had begun to open the door of my heart to him, the words just tumbled out until there was nothing left to say.

Having being given the go ahead by my extensive dialogue, Steve then shared how he had been in love with me for nearly a year and that he felt intoxicated by my very presence. I was amazed as he stumbled over his words, expressing the depth and strength of his feelings for me. His genuine desire to make me feel happy again was an unexpected addition to his already apparent charm and magnetism. I was utterly powerless to resist Steve any longer. We sat, intimately close to one another, relieved at finally being able to express our true emotions. At this moment, ripe with exquisite hunger and longing, Steve rose from his seat, gently but firmly took my hand, pulled me towards him, and then pushed me against the wall. Strong yet tender arms enveloped me, and I could feel each sinewy muscle in his body in its desperate longing to be wrapped around mine. His eyes were flaming with desire, and his sensual, full lips finally found their way onto my own. At first, our kisses were tender, gentle even, just brushing against each other as we enjoyed the anticipation of every scintillating, touching moment. But as our passion heightened, so did the force and vigour of our embrace. If you needed to light a cigarette, you could have lit it on the sparks flying from us! At this rate, we would get thrown out of the nightclub.

Suddenly, I felt my lungs were about to collapse and realised that I desperately needed to come up for air. As I opened my eyes and took a deep breath, I unglued my adhered lips from his. I looked around and noticed other couples, with their own partners, and the delicious delights they brought to each other's sensual taste buds. As I glanced around the northern club, I saw the usual goings on that you might expect. Disco divas cavorted provocatively, enticing those brave enough to watch but not touch. There was also the inevitable boozing and associated hilarious and animated behaviour. One guy, propped up at the bar, attempted to pick up his rapidly emptying beer glass only to completely miss the pint pot and grasp instead the generously proportioned bosom of the size 18 lady standing next to him. With one enormous swing of her outstretched forearm, she launched her ammunition, a bulging evening bag, at the wavering drunk, bellowing,

'Nobody ever touches me there. ' (Somehow, I don't think anyone ever had.)

'Sorry luv,' he groaned apologetically, as his alcohol saturated body tottered towards the floor.

Then there were the antics of the likely lads who genuinely believed they were the next 'strictly come dancing' champions. Quite how their jerky, uncoordinated, and unrestrained attempts at rhythmic oscillation could be perceived as entrancing or tantalising, I do not know. If 'night fever' was the reason for their appalling sense of tempo, I hoped for all our sakes that their temperature fell to within normal limits as soon as possible!

Having been amused by the comical arena that lay before me, the heat of our moment began to lose its intensity. Probably just as well. Who knows where it might have led! Steve then sat me next to him and held my hand, stroking my fingers with attentive devotion. My sparkling martini refreshed my parched and throbbing lips, and I knew then that I wanted more – more of this young, fervent young man who made me feel alive, who gave me affection, and who was totally infatuated with me. It had been so long since I had felt this way. I wondered why marriage seemed to take the fun out of a relationship.

A little while later, I found myself on the dance floor once more. Steve moved so easily, each move orchestrated perfectly in time to the heady rhythm. My own version was a little less harmonious, but by now I really didn't care. I was in love, and as the music whirled me around me, I became oblivious to anyone but my Steve. The words of the song 'One Night in Heaven' boomed from the speakers, and it felt most appropriate on our special evening together. If feeling loved, wanted, and desired by another is the essence of paradise, then I had floated into this wondrous place on my own cloud nine.

The fairytale night was over much too quickly. Cinderella had to leave the ball, but at least she had enjoyed the most amorous night of delectation and delight. No sex – it didn't seem important, since the feeling of being in love was more than enough.

So what now? Steve would be moving to France to start a new life. Cinderella might not see her prince again, but at least they had shared their secret, precious feelings, and desires with each other. They could revel in the luxury of knowing they had enjoyed one evening of love and devotion together. Perhaps that would be enough to see them through?

Chapter Four

When Will I See You Again?

*B*EFORE I KNEW IT, STEVE had left for France. We had decided not to write or phone because there was little prospect of us seeing each other again. Our time together had come and gone, and that was that. I just had to get over it.

But when Steve left for France, he took with him my sense of adventure and, so I believed, my only chance of ever feeling loved. What remained was the heavy weight of despair with the prospect of my own marriage. An emptiness and feeling of loss pervaded my thoughts. Having had a taste of life in magnificent multicolour, my life now returned to monotonous black and white. And having experienced the excitement, thrill, and delight of being with Steve on our evening together, the prospect of life without him seemed so dull, mundane.

Yet somehow I managed to survive. The days took on their usual routine. Work was as busy as ever and at least there time flew by. But as Friday approached, a foreboding came over me at the prospect of yet another humdrum weekend. Was this all there was to life? Work and monotonous weekends? Fortunately my children were oblivious to any of my thoughts. Indeed, they were very happy and settled, enjoying the innocence of a blissful childhood. If only as adults we could all stay in the comfort and safety of a land where time seems to stand still and there is always a 'happily ever after'. So what if I wanted to live in a fairytale where Cinderella had a fabulously romantic relationship with her Prince Charming? Isn't that what we as little girls are led to believe we should dream for? Perhaps that is why I felt so disappointed with my own marriage and my husband's apparent lack of attention. I understood it now – *he* wasn't Prince Charming after all!

After only a few short weeks came terrible news. There had been a dreadful car accident on a French country lane involving Steve and his brother. Steve's brother had come out of it very lightly, but Steve was not so lucky. He had multiple broken bones and a shattered hip, the result of being impaled on the gear stick. Trust Steve to have an accident that involved knobs, I thought! At least he was still alive. For several weeks, Steve was nursed in an outdated French hospital. No doubt he loved all the attention from the French nursing staff. His recovery was slow at first, and doctors were uncertain whether his hip would ever function properly again.

I hadn't dared hope for the news that came next. He was returning to England. His parents wanted him to be nearer home, where they could visit much more easily, so Steve was flown back to continue his recovery close to his friends and his family. I wasn't sure what to do. I desperately wanted to see him again, yet I was afraid that I would not be able to hide my feelings for him in front of others. Somehow I managed to summon the courage, and deceit, to arrange a visit with his parents. My first visit gave me quite a shock, as I wasn't prepared for the effect the accident had on him. He was pale, thin, and weak. Yet the fervent electric current that had sparked between us still tingled as before.

Steve's convalescence was steady. And after many weeks of T. L. C., physiotherapy, and sheer hard work, his hip regained its function. A huge scar was the only sign of the damage done by the offending gear knob.

But what was Steve going to do next? And more to the point, what was I going to do as a result? Steve was back in the country, fully functioning again but with no desire to return to France and his brother's 'Wacky Racers' approach to driving. Although I was thrilled at the prospect of Steve being here, I never would have had the courage to go on our date at the nightclub if he wasn't leaving the country. Neither would I have revealed the depth of my feelings for him if I thought it would lead to something more. However, deep in my subconscious I wanted as much as Steve was willing to give.

Girls like me, with my background and Christian beliefs, just didn't *do* affairs. 'There's no option but to get on with our lives, separately,' I repeated to myself. And in truth, there wasn't. I had had my moment of romantic indulgence; now it was time to get back to the real world. My husband was a good hardworking man who loved his children. What more could I ask for? The trouble was, I did ask for more. I wanted more adventure, more passion, and more of what we had started on our 'one night in heaven'.

I don't recall just how it happened, but we did see each other again. At first, it was just opportunistic moments – a quick kiss here, a martini and Fosters there. But as Steve's infatuation became more intense, so did my desire to be the other's idol. I was on such an emotional rollercoaster – one minute hurtling upside down on the loop-the-loop, the next, floating gently by on the Love Boat. No wonder I felt nauseous!

Perhaps what happened next changed everything. Our relationship so far had had its share of physical moments, but only consisting of romantic conversations, loving kisses, and passionate embraces. This may sound a little contradictory, but despite being utterly absorbed by Steve, I had not believed that I could actually make love with him. I was married to somebody else. It was just not like me even to think about going that far. But going 'that' far is exactly what we did. There's a line from a song that was most fitting: 'you're the teacher and I've come to school'. For I was the pupil at the school of hedonistic pleasure, and Steve was my teacher. Having only ever had one sexual partner, my experience was limited. Don't get me wrong, my husband and I had shared passionate times together, but all that seemed a long time ago. At the tender age of twenty, Steve seemed to possess more 'sexpertise' in his little finger than I had in my whole body. Wow! Never had I experienced carnal excess with such abandonment. It would have taken a whole fleet of 'earth movers' to create a similar 'orgasmic' effect! I didn't know that going 'that' far could be 'that' amazing. Not surprisingly I wanted more.

On one level, I was enthralled by what was happening. On another, I was disgusted with myself. A battle was going on – on one side, those champion warriors fighting to uphold all that is good and decent; on the other, those sturdy soldiers in pursuit of sensuality and emotional gratification. I was caught in the middle of the battlefield, artillery firing all around me. I didn't know which campaigner to side with. Steve decided to help with the decision making and asked me to leave my husband and live with him. He promised a life of love, affection, and excitement. What should I do? Could I just walk away from a marriage of eleven years, from a man who had tried to do his best by me, and from a belief system that told me this option was wrong, very wrong?

I had a mammoth decision to make – a life of safety, comfort, and boredom or a life filled with adventure, passion, and exhilaration. If I said 'yes' to the first option, a life of pretty much the same as it had been lay before me. If I said 'no' to the second option, I would never know what could have been. And having a secret affair whilst being married was not an option I could live with. I was hopeless at telling, let alone living, a lie. Well, what would you do?

Chapter Five

There's No Place like Home

*N*EVER IN MY LIFE HAVE I made such a difficult, draining, life altering decision. The battle between the champion warriors and sturdy soldiers seemed to go on forever. It consumed my thoughts. I was unable to concentrate or function at work. I must have appeared to be an absolute emotional wreck. My weight dropped by one and a half stones. Even my hair played its part by falling out! Stress can do funny things to a woman, but at least my figure had benefited.

After what seemed like a lifetime (actually only a couple of weeks), I had made my decision. I had considered all the facts with my mind, but it was my heart that won the day. The sturdy soldiers had overcome the champion warriors in their courageous battle to keep me on the side of all that's good and true.

Having made my choice, I had to tell my husband. Even as I write, the emotional pain surges back. I hadn't bargained for the agony that I was about to unleash on my unsuspecting husband. I thought he didn't care, that he didn't love me and that he wouldn't really miss me. It hadn't occurred to me that I would hurt him or his pride. It was insufferably heart breaking watching a grown man weep in excruciating torment. He pleaded with me to stay, questioning how it would affect the children. Was I capable of wreaking such cruel and distressing news on those I cared for? Obviously I was, because the only means of coping with my heart wounding behaviour was to harden my heart towards him. Despite his attempts to change my mind by bringing flowers, asking me to attend marriage guidance counselling, and offering to change, it was all too little, too late. There was no going back.

How either of us survived those last few weeks in the same house I do not know. Unbearable doesn't come close to describing it. I must have just closed the door on the part of my heart that had once been wondrously in love with my husband. How he managed to be in the same room with me I cannot imagine. Fortunately we managed to put on an act of civility for the sake of the children, and they were too young to notice the torment that was going on under their innocent noses.

Leaving was the saddest and most difficult event I had experienced. We were both in tears as we stood awkwardly in the hallway, the situation far too painful to attempt to make any conversation. I recall a sense of abject loathing at my uncharacteristic behavior towards Gary. Yet a force from within compelled me to do it anyway. As I look back, the irony is that I believed my husband had no feelings for me any more. The distressed expression across his face and the tears that ran down his cheek seemed to contradict this belief. On our wedding day in sunny June, eleven years previously, I could not have conceived that it would end like this. Where had it all gone wrong? Why had it failed? And why did I feel so much anguish? These were questions I *should* have been finding answers for now, but it would be many months before I would be in a stable enough state of mind to contemplate them.

So I left the house we had made our own and Gary slowly closed the front door. I think it was at this point that he closed the door on me. Who could blame him? I drove off to the little cottage Steve and I had rented. On my arrival, I burst into tears, not really believing I had walked out on my marriage. It was as if it was happening to someone else and I was watching them.

The children handled it all remarkably well. As I look back, I think they were oblivious to the seriousness of what was happening to them. As far as they were concerned, both their mum and dad loved them very much, but they were going to live with mum and her new friend. I think my husband knew he wouldn't be able to look after them on his own, and leaving them behind was not an option for me anyway. Wherever I went, they came with me. For my son, it must have seemed like having a big brother who liked having fun with him. At three years of age, my daughter merrily went along with whatever was happening around her.

Over the next few weeks, something indescribable happened. Certainly, it wasn't something that I had bargained for. Up until the point I had told my husband my intentions, my relationship with Steve had been truly enchanting, romantic, and utterly exciting. All that had changed now. Harsh reality had set in. My emotions swung between all consuming guilt at my actions and the warmth of feeling cherished and adored by my new lover and partner. If I thought I had been on an emotional rollercoaster before, it was nothing compared to this. This was more like being on a ship in a vicious storm where the vessel is tossed from port to starboard and the icy water causes cold and searing pain as its lashes down upon its victims.

Yet I was surprised at how much I had grown to resent the limitations that life with Gary had brought. Living with Steve did give me the opportunity to do certain things which Gary had disapproved of. During our holiday with Steve's brother in France, I was able to loose my artistic nature and have a tattoo. This was something I had contemplated for many years but which Gary didn't want me to have done. I knew exactly what I wanted and where I wanted it. Something tasteful and yet with a hint of sensuality, a rose on my shoulder was just the ticket.

Steve's brother knew of a tattoo artist in Bourges. An appointment was made for the following day. We went along and although this was something I had longed for, the tension I now experienced caused my heart to pound wildly. What if it hurt? What about HIV and Hepatitis? I wondered as I walked through the door. It was too late to be answering these questions because there in front of me was quite a surprise. Whilst I had never met a tattooist before and did not have any preconceived ideas about how such a person might look, I hadn't bargained for this. A Red Indian of French Canadian origin! Tall and thick set with strong dark hair and a rugged complexion, he had an imposing presence. To be truthful, I felt quite scared. Steve and his brother introduced me and then left me alone with the non English speaking native. 'You and your big ideas, look where they've got you now,' I chided myself. However, as I looked around, whilst Big Chief Indelible Ink prepared his treatment room, I noticed how spotless the shop was. The carefully placed displays and photographs of previous clients evidenced the fact that there was more to Big Chief than I had realised. Perhaps under his weathered skin lay a meticulous man of extreme cleanliness. I believed this to be the case.

Upon deciding whatever happened next there was no going back, I took my chances with the Big Chief. He beckoned me through into his room. Clutching the catalogue he had given me whilst I was waiting, I walked in and pointed to the picture I wanted and where it should go on my body. It was the rose I had foreseen in my mind's eye. Nervously I lay on the couch, face down and waited. At first the needle pricking wasn't too bad but gradually it became more and more painful, until eventually it was intolerable. Just as I was about to ask him to stop (how I could have done this in French I'm not sure) he sat me up and gesticulated that he had finished. What a relief. My ordeal was over. The rose was in situ and I had survived the Big Chief's magic.

During the following days, the tattoo was quite sore and bled intermittently. Steve was his usual kind and caring self. He nursed the wound carefully assuring me it would look beautiful once it healed. As he had several tattoos already he knew what to expect. And he was right. A week later, it did look lovely. The experience taught me that it is worth pursuing your dreams, even if there is some discomfort along the way. This lesson would become even more apparent as my relationship with Steve took its course.

Steve was so considerate, trying to make me happy, loving me, and showering me with kindness. He acted so sweetly that one look with those deep chocolate eyes could take me away from the turmoil I now felt. Certainly he could transport me to another world on our child-free weekends spending hours of indulgent passion as we became intoxicated with each other. Yet the feeling of guilt was relentless, as was the struggle to come to terms with what I had done. If I thought I could walk away from a marriage without any scars, without any pain and without what I suppose we call baggage, I was wrong. I had so miscalculated the emotional impact of a broken marriage, even though I was the one who held the sledgehammer in her hand and did the breaking. I was also the one who everybody blamed. Former friends, family, and church members now publicly shunned me, treating me with contempt. The burden was too much to bear.

My life had radically changed. A former well respected member of the community and church, I had been held in high regard. I was now the subject of gossip and labelled as nothing more than an adulterous woman of dubious repute. My parents did not want anything to do with me either. To be honest, I wasn't surprised and in a way it was a relief not to have to face them. The guilt and shame I experienced would have made it difficult for me to see them anyway. To make matters worse, my husband had now become involved with an old friend of ours. I felt as if I was losing my grip on the situation. Having been the one who called all the shots, I now had no power, no money, and very few friends.

As I grappled with the emotional mess I had landed myself in, I decided my only course of action was to go back. I arranged to speak with my husband and tell him I wanted to return. I was to call at the house the next evening. Parking my car on the drive of my former home felt quite surreal. The familiar surroundings clashed with the uncomfortable emotions that surged through my heart as my trembling finger rang the bell. Gary opened the door and solemnly beckoned me in. A tense unease presided as we stood and talked in the kitchen. I told him how unhappy I was, that I had made a huge mistake and that I wanted my life back. But it was too late. He had moved on. He had decided to get on with his life, and so he was. He could never trust me again. I had no place in his life anymore. It was over, and he was filing for divorce. He had decided there was no going back, not now.

Looking back, I suspect the only reason I wanted to return to my husband was that I wanted my old life back. At the time, however, all I knew was that I just wanted to go home. I remembered Dorothy in the film The Wizard of Oz repeating over and over, 'There's no place like home, there's no place like home.' Perhaps if I repeated it enough, I would find my own way home. Unfortunately, just like Dorothy, I had a sickening feeling that I would be trapped in an unfamiliar land for quite some time.

Chapter Six

I Want to Break Free

And that takes us back to the point at the beginning of my story. I felt utterly alone – my parents did not wish to see me, and neither did my former friends. Only two people were willing to stand by me at this terribly difficult time. Angela, a long time friend, and Irene, a work colleague, would prove to be angels in disguise! Steve continued to 'love me for the both of us'. Why weren't my spirits as high as a kite? After all, it's not every day that someone eleven years your junior finds you irresistible. Yet, somehow, the power of Steve's love for me and the excitement he had once given me had begun to wane. But what could I do? There really was no going back to my former life. Furthermore, by now Steve's family had made huge sacrifices to include me in their lives. The whole situation had been an unexpected shock for them, just as it had been for my husband. And just like him, they hadn't asked for this situation or wanted it. It really was quite a mess.

Emotionally I was all over the place. Oh yes, the grass may have seemed greener on the other side, and may have even been that way for a while. But now the reality was that the original lawn looked pretty lush. At least then, I wasn't riddled with guilt and self-loathing at the havoc I had wreaked on so many lives. One day, I spent the whole day in bed, curled up under the duvet like a small child. I was unable to get out and face the devastation I had created. I just wanted to hide from the unfamiliar world I now found myself in. I was overwhelmed with grief at the loss of my marriage. My husband had begun divorce proceedings, and I had to engage a solicitor. It was a situation I had not foreseen when my heart was hungering after another. I suppose that is what happens with greed, whether for food, approval, sex, or any other unbridled appetite: there is always a price to pay. For me, it wasn't the obesity that accompanies overeating but the emotional pain of a broken marriage and the all-consuming guilt that accompanies adultery. At least it accompanied me. Some people seem able to go after another's partner and truly believe they have the right to do so, Steve being one such person. I have found myself asking if it is possible to do this *and* possess a conscience. Steve certainly had a heart, but I'm not so sure about the state of his conscience. Perhaps Steve and others like him resort to casuistic, false reasoning. Maybe their sense of self is so grossly out of proportion that they are incapable of caring about another's pain. Some try to bury their conscience so deeply that they mistakenly believe it will never trouble them again. Others just ditch their value system for one that allows them to live with their actions. I certainly don't understand how anyone can do it, at least whilst maintaining one's self-respect.

Self-respect was something I had not experienced in a long time. The void it left behind was soon filled by guilt and self-loathing, dominating my entire emotional being. The pain and shame I had caused my husband, taking my children away from their father and throwing my parents' world into chaos, was simply too much to bear. How I survived those next few months I do not know. Decisions had to be made, but my mental state was not at all healthy, yet Steve relied heavily on me to hold our practical needs together. I had realised we needed to buy a house, as the rent was costing more than a mortgage. My husband was buying my share of our joint property, and at least there would be enough for me to use as a deposit on another house once that came through. So it was that Steve and I began to look for a home together. It wasn't easy, as we had very little in the way of earnings and mortgage companies found us to be a high risk.

By now, my rose tinted glasses had fallen off. Steve's love for me was strained under my permanent low mood and persistent difficult circumstances. I was also beginning to question whether or not I ever truly loved him. I still had strong feelings for him, but living with someone who has completely different values, beliefs, and interests is not an ideal situation. He still told me he loved, adored, and valued me, but this no longer had the same appeal. And great sex is just not enough in a relationship where one partner is consumed with guilt.

However, Steve continued to insist that his love was strong enough for us both. He assured me that our circumstances would improve once we were in our own home. I attempted to change Steve's smoking and drinking habits. He assured me he would stop, and he tried to – or at least he told me he had. Despite the apparent lies, his inexperience at handling finances, and his apparent lack of any real career prospects, I believed there was no alternative but to continue to hope and trust all would work out well in the end. How naive could I have been?

Although I had bought and sold many houses before, I had never experienced as many difficulties as I had with this one. The problems just kept piling up, and without my husband there to sort them out, I felt hopeless and helpless. The uncertainty became intolerable. I sank deeper and deeper into depression. On one occasion I had to be sent home from work because I couldn't handle the insurmountable difficulties with buying the new house. What a mess I had become. How had I ended up like this?

Eventually, after a multitude of 'phone calls and visits to the solicitor and the mortgage lender, we finally moved into the new house. I was delighted with our gorgeous three-bedroom cottage. With original beams, low ceilings, and wobbly walls, it oozed charm and character. It was also completely modernised, an ideal place, I thought, to make a home for Steve, myself, and the children. Perhaps our circumstances would improve now that we had our own home.

My children had a good relationship with Steve, although at times I found his behaviour could be volatile. In fact, this behaviour was one of my growing concerns. At this point, however, I chose to ignore this small questioning voice and plough headlong into creating some form of stable life for myself.

By now, Steve had asked me to marry him, and to be honest, I jumped at the chance. Although I was feeling unsure about our relationship, I didn't feel there were any real alternatives other than staying together. In any case, we now had a joint mortgage, so we were obligated to each other. One of the causes of my low mood was the prospect of being divorced and living with the disgrace that I perceived surrounded me. Neither was I comfortable with living together. For whatever reason, I just wanted to be married again, and respectable in my own eyes. Finally, it seemed as if normality was returning to my incredibly troubled world.

The children settled well at their new school, made good friends, and acclimatised well to the constantly changing circumstances thrust upon them. They really were little darlings! I do believe young children often accept life's complex and difficult situations much better than adults do. My two were certainly much more stable and balanced than I was at this time.

Steve and I had even visited a local church, where we talked with the minister about our circumstances. It could not have been easy for him to understand how we had arrived in our situation, yet he didn't judge us and later discussed our plans for marriage. On one occasion he questioned me, alone, as to whether I loved Steve and whether marriage was the right course of action. I insisted it was and assured him that it was what I wanted. As the words formed on my lips, however, a churning sensation was gurgling in my stomach. What did the unexpected rumblings mean? Why could I hear that faint questioning voice calling me again? I chose to ignore it, but the strange discomfort I felt would prove to be more significant than I had anticipated.

And so we continued to make our wedding plans. Steve was most excited because he had not been married before. I was very conscious that I had. Steve's family was happy for him and were busy contacting relatives and making their own preparations. We viewed several potential reception venues and finally found one that was suitable. The church was booked, and I bought a simple yet elegant wedding gown. Steve had asked a long time friend to be his best man and he had agreed. On chatting with me, he commented that I was 'so brave' to marry Steve. I wondered what he meant but I was too scared of what his answer might be. I sensed the same unease I had experienced before.

Shortly afterwards, on a crisp March afternoon, my eyes caught the sight of a wedding party emerging from the quaint village church across the road on the green. I gazed through the window at the bride and groom. I could hear their joy and happiness in their laughter and see it in their smiling faces and their close embrace, as they tenderly kissed for the camera. I imagined a similar scene on my forthcoming wedding day, but the more I pictured it in my mind's eye, the clearer the image became of a very different scenario. For the bride I foresaw did not look at all like the rapturously happy woman who was enjoying her special day on the village green outside my window. Neither was she smiling at her groom or laughing with the guests. For once, she would not enjoy being the centre of attention. But before I could work out why this should be, Steve entered the room. It was a good job he couldn't read my mind. Seeing the happy couple through the window, he asked if I was looking forward to our wedding. I hesitated, desperately searching for the answer I knew he wanted to hear but was unable to give, and swiftly fled the room.

Although at this time I didn't understand *why* I felt the way I did, I knew something was horribly wrong. That evening

Steve went out, as he often did, usually to meet up with friends. Whilst he was not at home, I did a great deal of thinking. Big questions needed asking. Chaos reigned in my thoughts and I experienced a deep sense of unease. I realised there was only one person who could help me with such an enormous task. I had recently started to talk with him again. I sat and prayed. Partway through my heavenly dialogue I rang my dear friend Angela, asked her to pray for me too, and explained why. She faithfully promised she would. As it turned out, she prayed with more emotion and gusto than she had ever before. God must have known we meant business. Though I knew it not at the time, so did He!

Having finished my prayerful conversation, I progressed from lying on the bed to sitting on the floor. As I thought over everything that had happened and the wide range of emotions I had experienced, I began to see things more clearly. I realised that I was only marrying Steve to make something very wrong right. Whilst I was still fond of Steve, I could see that I had stopped loving him a long time ago. Indeed, I wondered now if I had ever been in love with him at all. Was it possible that I had only been in love with the *idea* of being in love? Had I mistaken infatuation for real love? Had I become so desperate for love and affection that I had been blind to the truth? Was I only with Steve because I felt trapped and couldn't get out of the messy situation I had created? Sadly, my answer to all these questions was a resounding yes.

My thoughts became ever clearer. In my new understanding of the situation, I suspected that Steve's 'love' for me was probably infatuation and that at some point, it would wear off. After all, real love focuses on the *other* person, not on how they make *us* feel. According to 'The Message', (The Bible in contemporary language)

Love never gives up...cares for others more than for self... doesn't want what it doesn't have... love doesn't force itself on others, isn't always 'me' first, doesn't fly off the handle. Love doesn't keep score of the wrongs of others... or revel when others grovel. Love takes pleasure in the flowering of truth, puts up with anything...always looks for the best, never looks back but keeps going until the end. Love never dies.

If this is real love, why do we use the word so flippantly? More to the point, why had I? If only I had understood what love really meant when I had taken my wedding vows. If only I had realised that 'feeling' in love was about my own emotions, how *I* felt. This is a very different state of affairs from the *choice* and promise to 'love' another, which is about being and doing the best for *them*. I could see that whilst I had loved my husband, I had abandoned the commitment and selflessness that true love requires. In its place I had succumbed to what I falsely believed was the real thing with Steve. The sad fact is it was nothing of the kind. Perhaps phrases like "It makes me feel good with you in my life" and "I'm infatuated with you" would have been much more appropriate for me to use with Steve.

If only I knew then what I know now, none of this mess would have happened.

Yet it had happened, and I could see that even if I married Steve, I would never forgive myself for breaking up my first marriage and being the cause of the hurt and chaos that ensued. One of the downsides of living in a throwaway society is that there is a tendency to treat our marriages the same way we treat our mobile 'phones. When the feelings of newness and excitement have gone, when they no longer make the owner feel good about themselves, they are tossed aside for the latest model. I was one such culprit. I had been sucked in by this disposable attitude. I had treated my husband like an out of date mobile 'phone and become addicted to excitement, looking for someone who could 'ring my bell' and make me feel good inside. Instead of looking for a way to make my marriage work – by going to relationship counselling, perhaps – I had taken what seemed like the easy option. I had chosen to ditch it.

I concluded that whilst my first marriage might have failed anyway, abandoning a husband for another man was not the best way to handle a struggling marriage.

As these revelations gave me more and more clarity, I realised that I had been deceiving myself for many, many months. I knew what I had to do. My relationship with Steve had to end. I didn't know how I would manage, financially or practically, but what was most important to me now was my own peace of mind. In order for this to happen, I had to forgive myself for my actions and receive the forgiveness of an unconditionally loving God – a God who desperately longed for my reconciliation with him.

And so the confessions of this unfaithful heart allowed me to receive the forgiveness I so desperately sought. Almost immediately, something amazing happened. A colossal weight, one that had gradually made my life intolerable, simply and almost effortlessly fell away. In its place transcended a sense of serene calm and tranquillity. I was filled with pure joy and relief, two emotions I had not experienced since the whole affair had begun. I'm not sure how long I lay on the floor in a state of divine enjoyment, sobbing with a mixture of elation, solace, and indulgence in God's amazing grace. If heaven was anything like this, when my time came, I would relish the prospect of celestial dwelling! So many of us underestimate the importance and relevance of the spiritual part of our lives. For me, trying to cut out such a major part of my life had wreaked havoc on the rest of my being. As a result, chaos reigned, bringing a sense of intense emptiness and meaningless. However, now the balance was back, the relationship with my Heavenly Father was restored and this prodigal daughter had returned home. Like the lost son in Luke's gospel, who had not appreciated what he already had, I now truly valued my Father's love and approval. I would not choose to live without it again.

I learnt a great deal about forgiveness that night. I had falsely believed that forgiveness meant letting the offender off the hook or accepting that what had been done was okay. It was neither of these. In my case, forgiveness meant accepting full responsibility for my actions and their consequences. But it also meant that I did not have to carry the intolerable burden of guilt that had almost consumed me and caused me to make even more poor decisions. Little did I know it at the time, but there were those who would have preferred that my life be utterly miserable. In their eyes, I should have received my 'just desserts'. As well as learning about forgiveness, I realised that to be gracious towards those who are truly repentant, and even those who are not, is a wonderful act of human kindness.

Now that I had made the decision, it was as if I was standing at the other side of a door, one that had been there all the time but that I had been unable to see let alone open. Yet little did I know that through this doorway lay the solution to my complicated circumstances. And standing at *this* side of the door, my eyes could perceive the situation in a totally different light. I could see that a terrible mistake had been made but that there was finally hope for me, my children, and our futures. At last, I was free – free from the guilt and shame that had consumed me, free from the constraints of believing I could only be happy if loved by another man, and free to create a life of my own choosing.

Yes, I did want to be free, but my freedom had come at a high price and more had yet to be paid – a marriage already lost and another that now would not happen. Further pain lay ahead for Steve and his parents, who had finally given me their trust and showered me with kindness. How could I possibly contemplate causing them more distress? Yet not only did I contemplate it, but I began to work out what I was going to say to Steve and his parents. There was little time before Steve's return from the pub. I had to think quickly. Now back from my visit to paradise, the earthly practicalities seemed to weigh heavily. Being concerned that Steve's temper might get the better of him, I knew I would have to be as tactful as possible.

He actually took it quite well at first. Although rather shaken, he remained calm and composed, but I don't think he was entirely surprised. He knew things weren't right between us, so I guess the excitement of the wedding must have been carrying him along. After the shock had worn off and reality set in, his emotions took over. Once again I saw temper rear its ugly head. To make matters worse, he gave his parents the unpleasant news before I could, so what they heard was Steve's version of events rather than mine. I desperately wanted to apologise, to say how sorry I was for the distress and anguish my actions had caused them. They had been so gracious towards me, and look how I had repaid that kindness. Truly, they didn't deserve what had happened, and I wouldn't blame them for despising me. If only they would have let me speak with them, let me tell them how much I wished I could turn back the clock and wipe away all the emotional agony I had inflicted upon them. If so, perhaps they would have understood. But it was not to be. They refused to speak with me, and who could blame them?

By now, Steve was not handling the situation well. I found his behavior erratic and threatening which reassured me that my decision to stop the wedding was the right one. It was a real relief when he agreed to leave, but then one of his brothers joined in with the threats and I had to arrange to have my locks changed. I felt afraid and alone. How I would have survived the next few weeks without my two friends, I do not know. One of my angels in disguise, Irene, was a motherly figure at work. She had taken it upon herself to watch over me in the absence of my own mother. She was literally a Godsend, proving time and again the value of true friendship, supporting me when few others would. Everyone should have at least one of these angels in his or her life. Life can be so unbearably hard without them.

Finally, Steve began to see that my decision was for the best, for both of us. After many difficult conversations, we were able to part on much friendlier terms. I trust the whole episode had taught him a great deal about himself, his family, and true love. Years on, I heard he married and had a child. I do hope he has found the happiness and contentment he so desperately longed for.

Over the next few weeks I found myself back at the imaginary theme park many times, riding on the emotional rollercoaster. One of the real highlights was when my parents replied to my letter asking them to forgive me for everything I had put them though. I wasn't sure of the response I would receive, as it had been over a year since I had had any contact with them. I needn't have worried. Mum wrote back with genuine delight and relief that the affair was now over. My parents wanted to see me, and so we arranged to meet at a local restaurant for a meal. I was nervous, not sure whether I would get a long lecture from my Dad. As with the letter, I needn't have worried. We had a warm and wonderful reunion. In fact, we virtually carried on from where we had left off a year previously. Of course they had questions, but they were asked with real concern and affection. By the end of the meal, I think we had all learned something about ourselves, each other, and relationships. The memories of this occasion have remained with me ever since, and they are memories I still deeply cherish.

My next task was to sort out my financial situation. Faced with a mortgage I was unable to pay on my part-time wage, there was nothing to do but find another job to fit around my existing hours. I was fortunate and managed to pick up a position in a local nursing home, where I could work some day and nightshifts to suit my schedule. Although it meant some days I would have to work all day and then all night, it was the answer I had been looking for. Anyway, a bit of hard work never hurt a girl, did it?

My son and daughter, yet again, adapted tremendously well to another new situation, now as the children of a single mum. They thrived at school and didn't appear affected by their mother's chaotic antics. I was truly thankful that they were developing into such remarkable young people. In fact, all these experiences would actually help them become more grounded and level headed as they grew older. However, I don't recommend my course of action as a means to teach your children life lessons. That my own children would turn out to be so remarkable was the result of good fortune, good management, and divine intervention!

Gradually, my life began to take on a new sense of normality. It certainly wasn't a normal I had anticipated one year before or one that I had wanted. However, it was one which I was now grateful to have. It could have turned out so differently, with even more mess and even more disastrous consequences.

I had a roof over my head, two amazingly happy and resilient children, great friends, and a future I could look forward to.

Despite my newfound contentment, my husband's remarriage was difficult. Shortly after I had stopped the relationship with Steve, I once again pleaded with my husband to let me return. I believe it was for the right reasons, but by this time he had announced his engagement. I think he felt I was just being difficult and trying to spoil his new life. I somehow thought that he would see how I had changed and how repentant my spirit was. And yes, I know, why did I think he would respond any differently?

Chapter Seven

Starting Over

I COULDN'T BEAR THE THOUGHT OF my ex-husband remarrying and me being on my own. Feeling vulnerable and quite alone, in desperation I responded to a lonely hearts advert in the local paper. Surely someone would find me attractive and want to be with me. Even though I had instigated the breakdown of my marriage, I hadn't expected my ex-husband to be the first to remarry.

Nervously I rang the number of a guy who sounded like my type, someone looking for friendship and long term commitment. I was put through to a disapproving secretary, which wasn't quite what I had expected. But before I knew it, she had connected me to her charming, deep voiced, and smooth talking boss. He sounded like a decent sort and appeared interested in me, so we arranged to meet in the bar of a well known hotel one lunchtime. As the day approached, I certainly felt a little anxious. You hear so many stories about this type of thing. At least we were meeting in a very public place, and in daylight. Putting any negative thoughts aside and hoping for the best possible outcome, I pulled up outside the hotel. Appearing as cool and confident as I could, I elegantly strolled into the bar and our rendezvous point. Inside, waiting for me, was a tall, dark haired, professional looking gentleman who warmly greeted me. After the initial pleasantries, he asked me to tell him all about myself. Not having done this before, and feeling very apprehensive, I blurted out my whole story! How stupid. What was I thinking of? I had either put him off completely or given him a vibrant green light.

It turned out to be the exact signal he had been looking for. He must have thought his luck was in, as he began to reveal the sort of woman he was after. I was filled with disgust and dismay as he calmly proceeded to tell me about his wife, his nine month old daughter, and the relationship with his mistress of many years, which had recently come to a mutual end. As I was unable to respond, which I attribute to shock, he continued, inviting me to become his new mistress, offering me a life of affection, luxurious gifts, and excitement! I know I was lonely and vulnerable, but I wasn't that desperate! To this day, I wish I had kicked him where it hurts, but being too stunned and too polite, I told him directly that I wasn't interested, at which point he attempted to blackmail me, saying that if I told anyone, he knew where I lived! No wonder his secretary disapproved.

So much for appearing to be a 'decent' sort. My journey home was filled with the realisation that it was a scary world out there. I had not at all enjoyed my encounter with the slimy beast from the cess pit of humanity. 'Some men can be so despicable', I told myself. My sympathy lay with his wife and daughter. Recovering from my own painful divorce had made me realise there was no way I could be the cause of someone else's. I also learnt that it wasn't a good idea to tell the world about my past. I certainly wasn't going to make that mistake again. Well, at least I wasn't going to tell anyone I didn't yet trust.

Despite this eye-opening experience, I determined not to be put off men for good. So, 'phone in hand, I called another 'lonely heart' to discover whether I could find true love. This time, my date proved much more promising, a divorced accountant. Gentle and considerate, he planned to take me to a country park not far from where we lived. We arranged to meet there, and as the sun smiled down on us, we chatted and shared stories, although this time I was much more cautious with the details I passed on. I was definitely learning. My heart swelled with enjoyment whilst being in the company of an educated, considerate man who seemed to find me quite appealing. All was going well until he nonchalantly placed his arm around my waist, touching my bare skin beneath the crop top I daringly sported. To my surprise, I felt the tiny hairs covering my body stand to attention with distaste. My stomach churned in uncertain fear of what might follow. How could this be? The setting was suitably stunning and I liked the guy I was with, yet I was filled with strange repulsion as his flesh touched mine. It certainly wasn't the fault of my companion, for he had shown nothing but consideration and gentlemanly behaviour. Thinking quickly, I had to make some excuse to remove his arm from my middle, so I bent down to take in the scent of a wild rose. That aromatic flower didn't know how relieved I was to take in its fragrance! As I stood again, free of any offending limbs, I took my date's hand and firmly held it. I could cope with that. At least this way I could control what he did with it. Hand in hand, we completed our scenic stroll. I don't think he was any the wiser.

My unexpected reaction proved that I wasn't ready for any sort of physical contact or serious relationship. This surprised me, as I thought I was. Was my wanting a date a knee jerk reaction to my ex-husband's wedding? I realised that the *fear* of being unloved was actually worse than *being* unloved. Being with someone for the sake of it would not solve this conundrum. Anyway, just because a bloke didn't love me at this moment in time didn't mean I wasn't lovable, lovely, or worthy of love. At least I had learned something else about myself, something positive, from the second 'lonely hearts' encounter. Needless to say, I didn't arrange to see the accountant again, nor anyone else for that matter.

On the day my ex-husband married, I was in rather a depressed mood. I accept that our divorce had been caused largely by my own actions, but the situation that followed was one I hadn't bargained for, one in which the emotional power had been snatched away by others. It was an outcome which filled me with deep regret.

I realised I was experiencing bereavement at the death of my marriage. It would be many months before I would not feel intense sadness about it. I believe that viewing it in this light was an emotionally healthy way to handle it, to understand why it was such a painful process. It was as if I were being torn limb from limb. It wasn't just the loss of what I had had; it was the loss of all the hopes and dreams I had anticipated experiencing with my husband. The loss of the love and affection of a man who had known me as a teenager, the joy of seeing our children grow into young adults and enjoying time together in our older years, visiting new and exciting places. It is no surprise that so many find divorce so painful. It isn't just the *physical* loss of your partner; the emotions that accompany it can be just as tormenting. Whether rejection, guilt or betrayal, the heart is damaged, seemingly forever.

For my ex-husband and his new partner, their marriage was a happy, blissful, even ecstatic day. For me, a part of my life had ended, a part that I was not ready to let go of. How the tables had turned. Again, I spent much of the day in tears of regret and emotional torment. It's funny that we picture none of this when an exciting and all encompassing affair begins.

Yet, by the end of this traumatic day, and with the support and encouragement of my minister's compassionate wife, I had managed to work through more issues. I had been carrying so many heavy bags around with me, it was a wonder I was able to remain upright! At least I was learning I could begin to put them down, one by one. As a result, in time, I was able to put my past well and truly behind me. There was no going back. Everything had changed and there was nothing I could do about it. I had no option but to let go and move into the future, even though it was totally unknown. Yes, it was scary, and yes, it would take courage, but I was finally ready to face life, full on, by myself. In my night of redemption, spent on the 'celestial' carpet, and after forgiving myself for what I had done, I had taken the first step. Letting go of the past and beginning to make my life work for me was the second one, a further step on my precarious journey to discovering who I was always meant to be.

Chapter Eight

Single

And so it was that by the end of June, the 'new' me began to emerge. Now financially secure and living independently in the cottage originally purchased with Steve, I was able to continue working on my own character development. So much was whirling around in my mind. I spent many a night curled up in bed, reading, questioning, and working out why I had made such a dreadful mistake. I resolved to discover the answer to ensure it never happened again. The prospect of so much pain and emotional agony being inflicted on those involved was just unbearable.

As I worked through my questions, my thoughts were drawn back to my childhood. As I relived many of the events and feelings associated with my past, I saw a picture of a girl whose parents loved her deeply. When this child was small, the affection and attention came freely to her, but as she developed into a headstrong young woman, her parents found her difficult to handle. The girl wrongly interpreted this to mean that her parents did not like her, so she turned to anyone who could show her the love and attention she craved. Consequently, boyfriends filled the gap. Quite innocent relationships really, but driven by a strong desire for approval and the need to feel good about herself. No wonder this girl married so young. Even though the choice was anchored in love, once she no longer felt valued, appreciated, and wanted, the same old feelings of low self-worth and poor self-image reared their unsavoury heads once again.

It was becoming clearer and clearer. I had made a mistake, yes. It was a mistake of incalculable proportions and an enormously public one, but a mistake nonetheless. Despite what so many people had said about me, I wasn't a wicked woman, a 'tart', or a 'man-eater'. I was a woman who had placed unreasonable demands on her husband, demands that no partner could have met, much less one whose love for me seemed to be waning. Instead of working these issues through with my husband, I had become so desperate for love, affection, and appreciation that I allowed myself to succumb to the charms of another. It is worth reiterating how my low level of self-worth had driven me to seek love and approval elsewhere. I had been on a lifelong mission to search out anyone who would make me feel better about myself. What an impossible quest! And how unfair to expect a husband to be responsible for his wife's happiness.

What a revelation! What a relief and what a boost to my flagging confidence. Finally I could see that the only person's approval I really needed was my own. All this time I had been in search of happiness, I'd been looking in the wrong places. I hadn't realised it, but the key to my happiness lay inside *me*! Instead of looking to others to 'make' me feel good, all I needed to do was work at building my own self-belief, self-worth, and self-esteem. Taking responsibility for my own happiness and future was a monumental step for me. In fact, it was the third step on the ladder to becoming the 'real me'. This followed the forgiveness I experienced in my bedroom (my carpet experience, as I call it), and my letting go of the past.

I was quite surprised at what happened next; you might be taken aback too. I actually began to like myself. Having taken steps one, two, and three, I now had a totally different perception of who I really was. And when I delved within the depths of my heart, I knew I was a loving, kind, generous, and honest person. There were a whole host of qualities I loved about myself, and others that I was proud of. All these years of being so hard on myself, focusing on what I wasn't instead of what I was, had caused me to have a faulty impression of the 'real' me. No wonder I liked this new woman – she was amazing!

As the weeks went by, I became more and more emotionally whole. I realised that, since childhood, my faulty thinking had resulted in faulty behaviour. There is a parallel here with medical problems. Instead of dealing with the root cause, I was constantly addressing my symptoms. Just as with an undiagnosed and untreated medical condition, the symptoms kept coming back, with a vengeance, resulting in devastating consequences. At last, I had discovered the remedy for the root of the problem. And, boy, was I applying the treatment liberally!

The pace at which I was recovering, growing, and developing astounds me to this day. My self-respect restored, my confidence and self-image soared. Colleagues commented on it, as did an elderly gentleman at my local church. One Sunday morning, I recall him saying, 'The lady who sits at the front is a very different one from the woman who used to sit at the back. Her countenance has a very different appearance now'. It was an accurate description, reflecting the inner changes that had taken place.

A real sense of being liberated encapsulated my thoughts. An independent woman was not something I had ever aspired to be or believed possible. Yet that was exactly what I had become. My two part-time jobs enabled me to be financially secure, although funds were very tight and I didn't qualify for any state benefits to assist with the children. I felt proud of the fact that I could manage and care for the children on my own.

Small accomplishments made such a difference to my confidence, such as the time the plug on my hairdryer blew up. When I had been married, my husband would have sorted it out for me, and before that, my dad. Now, there was no one on hand to help me. So, armed with a screwdriver, new plug, and instructions, I set to it. The screwdriver had the wrong shaped end, the screws were so small they kept falling out of the holes, and the instructions made no sense at all, not to me anyway. Eventually, with the correct headed screwdriver, I mastered this small but intensely annoying electrical device. I showed it who was boss! The new plug attached, I set about drying my hair only to realise that it had already dried. By now I looked like an extra from Scary Movie, but at least *this* extra could tell the difference between a cross head and a flat headed screwdriver!

After the electrical socket incident, I turned my newly acquired skills to the car. I could drive very well. In fact this was one area where my confidence had always been in plentiful supply. Perhaps I should have been a rally driver rather than a nurse. Driving a car and putting petrol in posed no problems whatsoever, but ask me to perform any maintenance and I didn't have a clue. So, at my next visit to the garage, I asked one of the mechanics to show me how to check the oil and tyre pressures. After locating the lever for the bonnet (yes, I'm ashamed to say I didn't know where that was either!) we opened it and he explained what to do. Whilst it was a bit greasy, I understood his instructions and regularly kept an eye on it after that. The tyre pressures proved relatively easy to check, and yet again my confidence experienced a growth spurt. This car maintenance lark wasn't so difficult after all. I think the guys shroud it in mystery to make themselves look good!

After that, I even tackled the use of a drill, to erect some shelves in my daughter's bedroom. Talk about having a life of its own! As I gently pressed the 'on' button down, the drill leapt about the wall like a deranged cat with me hanging on to its tail! What an experience that turned out to be. However, determined not to be beaten, I resolved to show this 'boring' creature that I would not be defeated. Armed with determination and perseverance, I waged war on my electrical enemy, and after a long and arduous battle, it surrendered. The shelves were in place and, despite being a little wonky, they looked fabulous!

There was actually far more learning going on than I realised with these newly acquired practical skills. They showed me how I had imposed many self-limiting beliefs upon myself — not only on my ability to perform practical tasks, but more importantly, on the perception I held about myself. This restrictive thinking had cost me dearly, as I looked back over recent events, but I was now realising that I really could achieve, and become, anything I set my mind to. All I needed was determination, perseverance, and a willingness to change. Wow, this really was life changing stuff. However, without the support of good friends, who helped with childcare, I could not have managed practically. Whilst becoming more and more independent, I was not an island. Solid, dependable friendships were important to me and vital to my day to day functioning. When John and Paul wrote, 'I get by with a little help from my friends', they certainly knew what they were talking about.

By now, things were running smoothly and life had a calmness about it. This was something I was especially thankful for after the turbulent previous twelve months. As I felt more and more settled, my thoughts began to run ahead to my future. I even started a pension scheme to provide for my retirement. So, in practical terms at least, I planned as well as I was able to at that time. But I did begin to wonder whether my future would be spent alone. Most of the single women I knew devoted their whole lives to finding 'Mr Right'. I didn't want to live my life the same way. I remember one particular occasion, whilst in the shower of all places, I battled with this very dilemma. Could I really face the rest of my life on my own? To be honest, the prospect terrified me. I knew deep down that I did not want that. Yet I truly desired to enjoy my life without the constraints of feeling incomplete, without a man by my side. If I had a relationship, I wanted it to be filled with commitment, passion, humour, and fun. In truth, I wanted a union with two whole, complete people, whose hearts were totally captivated by each other. I wasn't sure if this was possible, but as I contemplated this conundrum, I decided that I would not settle for anything less. It was either the man of my dreams or no man at all. Whatever the outcome, I resolved to make my future a great one. And do you know something? Having reached that decision, I felt fantastic! Whatever happened I couldn't lose!

Over the summer months, I revelled in the freedom that my newfound self-discovery had brought me. Having felt the years pile on as the result of the stress my affair had caused, I now felt them gently falling away as I relaxed into being, how shall I say, me. The woman that had been married previously was a very different one from the passionate creature that had followed her impetuous emotions. And the person that had emerged since was as different again, still passionate, but now about life.

Of course, my personality was still the same; gregarious, a little loud, rather extravagant, smiley, and blonde! However, my newfound knowledge had enabled me to acquire a whole host of new characteristics. Confidence, enriched self-esteem, increased self-worth, and a new outer image too. Having worked so diligently on the 'inner' me, I decided I would like the 'outer' me to reflect the improvements I had made. So I saved really hard and arranged to have my 'colours' done. The result was astonishing. From my top to my bottom (or should that be my toes?) the consultant revealed a side of me I didn't know existed. It was incredible. She taught me to recognise which colours and shades brought warmth and freshness to my face. The style and colour of my hair, clothes, accessories, and make-up were fashioned to reveal my best features whilst disguising the least flattering. It wasn't rocket science, but it was awfully clever. I haven't looked back since and would recommend it to any woman who wishes to make the most of herself. It certainly worked wonders for me. My confidence improved even more, and I felt more attractive than I had ever done. Although I wouldn't have believed I could say this of myself, I thoroughly loved being the 'new me'.

The end of August brought a two-week holiday with the children. Due to our limited finances, we had planned to have days out rather than to go away. We thoroughly enjoyed ourselves and each other's company. My son took it upon himself to be the 'man' of the house and looked after us. My daughter just engrossed herself in whatever we chose to do. It was a heart warming time that drew us closer together as a family. We even acquired two gorgeous kittens, one for each of my children. What fun and joy they brought us, as well as completing our happy home. My life had taken on a new and very different 'normal' from the one I had experienced when I was married. Had I known then that this new life would become my 'normal', I would have been horrified. But instead of horror, I felt comfortable and relaxed with my alternative lifestyle.

And so it was that the summer of 1996 ended on a harmonious note – my self-respect restored, my confidence growing, and my self-worth and self-image at an all time high. Who would have believed it possible to have such contentment and happiness after everything I had put myself and my family through? Yet it was possible. And I was living proof! But my story was far from over; indeed, it was just the beginning. Because more, much more, was about to descend into my comfortable world. Over the bank holiday weekend, I went away with a group of people from my local church. I was so looking forward to it, company with others in the stunning setting of the North Yorkshire moors, bliss. It proved to be a weekend that I would never forget. A certain gentleman was about to walk into my life and turn it completely upside down. Just as I was getting used to the new order of things, it was all about to change, yet again.

What lay in store this time I could not have believed possible. I was about to embark on another incredible journey; a journey that would take me to vibrant and exciting lands. A new world that would herald the exquisiteness of true love and the inextinguishable hunger of inflamed passion. Once inside this garden of paradise, a union of two enchanted hearts would deliver limitless pleasure, delight, and contentment as they shared their lives as soul mates. Yet this Eden would also take me through the valley of death twice over and result in even more heartbreak and pain, the depths of which would cause a sadness never known before.

These challenging experiences, ranging from sheer ecstasy to utter despair, would continue to shape me into the woman I am constantly evolving into. Little did I know that what lay ahead would be an adventure of a lifetime, taking me into unexplored territory. And like all pioneers, the trailblazer must lead the way, clearing a new path and venturing well outside of their comfort zone. My safety net was about to be burned, forever!

A personal note to you from Alison

Having read my story, you may be able to identify with the journey I have travelled. I would like to remind you of the three simple steps I took on the way to becoming a more confident, self assured and contented woman. As a result of these humble beginnings, my journey has enabled me to become, and achieve, far more than I ever believed possible. Consequently I have gone on to train as a Life Coach and Image Consultant, positively impacting the lives of many women. You too can have an amazing life filled with infinite possibilities if you dare to take that very first step. My desire for you is to become *all* you are capable of being and doing. So, be encouraged to take these simple actions and start your own adventure of a lifetime!

1. Forgiveness of yourself and others

Learn to love and like yourself, *just as you are*. Don't wait until you *feel* deserving or others think you are good enough.

Accepting yourself means that you accept you as *you*. It doesn't mean you have to like everything about yourself. Give yourself permission to accept yourself as you are, warts and all. From this point you can begin to forgive your own imperfections and start to work on changing your character for the better.

When it comes to forgiving others, it is vital for your own well-being. Holding onto unforgiveness is rather like eating a poisonous apple, hoping the other person will die. Unchecked, unforgiveness will lead to resentment and bitterness. This will gnaw away at you, negatively affecting your emotional, mental and ultimately your physical health. Remember forgiving someone else doesn't mean that they have 'got away with it' or that it was okay to hurt you. Forgiving them means that they do not have any hold on your future or your happiness. You can choose to let the offence go and maintain your dignity and self respect. Leave them to face the consequences of their wrong doing.

2. Letting go of the past

This simply enables you to move into your future without the constraints of old events holding you back. A technique that can help is to make a list of any old unpleasant event, offence, and negative or faulty thinking. Next, take a bag, any sort from plastic supermarket carrier to the latest designer label, and place, inside, the list you have made. See this as an outward sign that you are ditching the past. You now have a choice; to leave the bag behind or take it with you wherever you go. Many of us carry so many of these 'bags', we are weighed down by them all, and no wonder. Life is much lighter and simpler when we choose to let them go and leave them behind. We are then free to embrace our future and make it a great one.

3. Taking responsibility for one's own happiness and future

For many, there is a sense of the haphazard when it comes to life working out well or not. It certainly hadn't occurred to me that I had the power to shape my own future. I truly believed that my preconditioning, my upbringing and life events had more control than my own mind! How foolish and yet what a familiar story. We do not have to be restricted by the values and beliefs of our parents, peers or colleagues. We do not have to be limited by where we grew up, how much money our parents earned or what happens *to* us. We can CHOOSE what happens *within* us. We can CHOOSE to think and believe whatever we want. We can CHOOSE our own futures and happiness and plan accordingly. When we free ourselves of faulty thinking and open our minds to the possibility of what could happen if we choose, believe and then act, our dreams truly can become a reality!

Lavishly yours,

Alison x

About the Author

Alison L. Tinsley RGN Dip LC (Inst LC) Image Stylist

A Registered General Nurse for almost twenty years, Alison's life took a change of direction shortly after her decision to assist women in their quest for more confidence, more happiness and a more fulfilled life. Having learnt so much from her own challenging life experiences, Alison went on to train as a Life Coach and Image Stylist. Alison has established a successful coaching business and has set up the innovative Lavish Ladies Club, (group coaching/image/style), runs a variety of coaching and style workshops and writes for the e-magazine Lavish Living. She is regularly on BBC radio, and has been featured in the Daily Express and Yorkshire Post.

For more information or if you would like to contact Alison regarding Lavish Lifestyle Consulting or speaking engagements visit her website at www.lavishladies.co.uk

Printed in the United Kingdom by
Lightning Source UK Ltd., Milton Keynes
138265UK00001B/45/P